FAMOUS MOVIE MONSTERS™

MEET THE
WOLF MAN

The Rosen Publishing Group, Inc.
New York

R. K. RENFIELD

To my father, who always howled when the moon was full

Published in 2005 by The Rosen Publishing Group, Inc.
29 East 21st Street, New York, NY 10010

First Edition

Library of Congress Cataloging-in-Publication Data

Renfield, R. K.
Meet the Wolf Man/by R.K. Renfield.—1st ed.
    p. cm.—(Famous movie monsters)
Filmography: Includes bibliographical references and index.
ISBN 1-4042-0274-9 (lib. bdg.)
1. Wolf man (Motion picture) 2. Werewolf films—History and criticism.
I. Title. II. Series.
PN1997.W598R46 2005
791.43'72—dc22

                                                    2004020488

Manufactured in the United States of America

On the cover: Lon Chaney Jr. as the Wolf Man.

CONTENTS

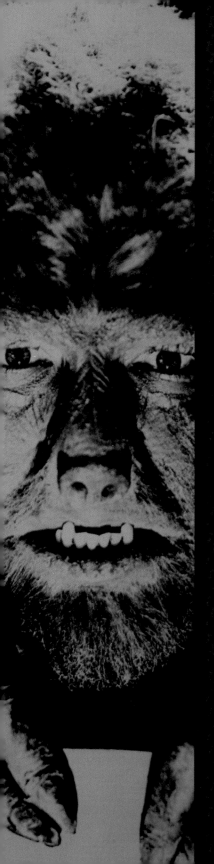

CHAPTER 1

THE WOLF MAN

At one time, people thought that werewolves walked among us by day, only to hunt us mercilessly by night. Although most people now dismiss werewolves as nothing more than legend or myth, there are still some places where people stay inside during the full moon. Superstition is still a powerful thing in these remote places, and for good reason—the supernatural is never farther away than the woods at the edge of town.

Information about werewolves can be found in libraries throughout the world. There is one library in particular, a library with shelves full of dusty volumes of mysterious writing, located in a castle somewhere in Europe. If you should find yourself there, you might come across an encyclopedia volume that contains the following entry:

LYCANTHROPY. (Werewolfism). A disease of the mind in which human beings imagine they are wolf-men. According to an old LEG-END, which persists in certain localities, the victims actually assume the physical characteristics of the animal. There is a

Lon Chaney Jr. *(right)*, the actor who played Larry Talbot, was much taller than Claude Rains *(left)*, the actor who played Larry's father, Sir John Talbot. In this scene, Larry talks with his father. Note that Chaney sits on the edge of the table in order to minimize the height difference between himself and Rains.

small village near TALBOT CASTLE that still claims to have had gruesome experiences with this supernatural creature.

*   *   *

Talbot Castle is nestled in the countryside of northern Europe. Larry Talbot, the next in line to inherit Talbot Castle and its surrounding countryside, is being chauffeured to meet his long-estranged father, Sir John Talbot. He hasn't seen his father for many years, and when they finally meet, their conversation is awkward. They discuss the tragic circumstances of Larry's homecoming: his older brother has been killed in a hunting accident. Larry is happy to reconnect with his father and has no reservations about leaving his life as an engineer to look after his father's estate.

The next day, Larry heads into town to meet his new neighbors. The town is small and peaceful, with a number of quaint shops and well-dressed people out shopping. Larry wanders into an antique store, where he meets the ravishing Gwen Conliffe, who works behind the counter. A flirtatious Larry purchases a cane from her store while trying to make a date with Gwen for the evening. The cane has a silver head, shaped like a wolf, with a pentagram engraved on it. When asked why the cane's head is in the shape of a wolf, Gwen explains the legend of the werewolf. She then recites an age-old poem:

> *Even the man who is pure of heart*
> *and says his prayers at night*
> *May become a werewolf when the wolfsbane blooms,*
> *and the autumn moon is full and bright.*

Larry laughs off the poem, although he'll come to believe in werewolves soon enough.

That night, Larry and Gwen, accompanied by Gwen's friend Jenny, set out for the gypsy camp at the edge of town to get their fortunes told. Night is beginning to fall, and a heavy fog swirls along the ground. Jenny notices some wolfsbane in bloom and repeats the poem Gwen recited earlier. With his new cane tucked under his arm, Larry smiles uneasily.

A gypsy fortune-teller named Bela meets them at the edge of the camp and agrees to read their palms and tell

Bela Lugosi's *(right)* bizarre charisma made him one of the sought-after horror stars in Hollywood. Seen here in his role of Bela the fortune teller, he delivers grim news to Gwen's friend Jenny. A talented and eccentric actor, Lugosi is most remembered for playing the title role in *Dracula*.

their fortunes. Jenny goes first. Instead of seeing the future in her palm, however, the old gypsy sees something strange—a pentagram, the sign that a werewolf sees on his next victim! The gypsy immediately lets go of her hand, unable to continue with the fortune-telling. Jenny is terrified by the horror she sees in Bela's eyes. She pleads with Bela to tell what he sees, but he cannot. Frantically, he begs Jenny to leave at once—she must run away!

Meanwhile, outside the camp, Gwen is explaining to Larry that his flirting is useless. She is engaged to be married. Suddenly, they hear Jenny's screams piercing the woods. Larry runs in the direction of the screams and sees an enraged wolf tearing at Jenny's lifeless body. Larry wrestles with the beast, eventually throwing it to the ground and furiously beating it to death with his silver-headed cane. Although Larry has killed the wolf, he has also been bitten a number of times. Exhausted, he staggers toward Gwen and collapses.

The next morning, Larry awakes in his bed. His father enters with a doctor and a police inspector. They tell Larry that Bela the gypsy's lifeless body has been discovered, and it appears that he was beaten to death! Next to the body, Larry's silver-headed cane was discovered. Larry pleads with the officer—he is not a murderer! He only fought with a wolf that had attacked a young woman.

The officer then informs Larry that there was no sign of a wolf, only the gypsy's mangled body. With evidence against him mounting, Larry tries to show them the wolf's bite wounds on his body, but they've inexplicably healed.

When the police officer leaves, Larry asks his father about werewolves. Sir John explains that werewolfism, or lycanthropy, is a condition that brings out the natural evil that dwells in people and that it exists only in their minds. He brushes aside the notion of actual werewolves as a mere superstition. Confused and afraid, Larry is not sure what to believe—although deep down, he knows that something evil is dwelling inside of him, and it's only a matter of time before it comes out.

Alone in his room that night, Larry worries that his future has something terrible in store for him. Night has fallen and a full moon has begun to rise. Soon, he notices that his shoes feel uncomfortable. He takes them off, only to see that his feet are growing and sprouting thick, black hair. Taking off his shirt, Larry finds that the thick hair is growing all over his body as well. There is nothing Larry can do to stop this strange transformation.

Later that evening, a hairy beast stalks through the trees and tombstones of a graveyard. Through the fog, the creature eyes a man digging a grave. The gravedigger doesn't even have time to scream before the monster's hulking form bears down upon him!

Later, the townspeople discover the grave digger's mangled body. A hunting party gathers to go on a manhunt for the killer, which they believe to be a wolf from the surrounding countryside. Armed with guns and torches, the hunting party searches the forest, but they are unable to find the creature.

The next morning, Larry is sleeping soundly in his bed. However, muddy footprints lead from the window of his room to his bed. When Larry wakes up, he frantically wipes away the footprints, frightened of what they might mean. It's Sunday, and Larry and his father head to church. Larry tries to join the service, but he freezes when he sees the congregation. An invisible force does not want him there and compels him to turn and flee.

Meanwhile, the hunting party continues to hunt for the killer wolf and sets deadly traps throughout the woods. They know that the longer they take to find the creature, the more people will die.

Later that night, the werewolf is stalking through the forest when a bear trap clamps down on its leg. The monster writhes in pain, but is unable to get free. The hunting party hears the beast's cries and closes in. The werewolf continues to struggle with the trap's iron jaws, but it is no use. There's no escape.

As the monster helplessly lies on the forest floor, an old gypsy woman appears. She calms the beast, and the werewolf changes back to its human form—it's Larry! The old gypsy woman helps Larry free himself from the trap and then she mysteriously disappears again. When the men in the hunting party come upon him, they have no idea what transpired. They think that Larry is just out hunting for the killer as well and accidentally stepped in one of their bear traps.

After the hunting party passes, Larry sneaks off to the antique shop to tell Gwen he must flee the village. By now, Larry has no doubt he carries a dark secret. He confesses to Gwen that he's a werewolf and that he's killed people. But during his pleas, the mark of the pentagram appears on Gwen. She will be his next victim!

Filled with despair, Larry runs through the night until he reaches Talbot Castle. There, his father steadfastly refuses to believe that Larry is the creature from ancient legend. He ties his son to a chair, telling him that he'll be cured in the morning. As he turns to leave and lock his son inside, Larry makes him take the silver-headed cane along just in case.

The Wolf Man crouches over the fresh corpse of his latest victim—the town's grave digger. The sets used in *The Wolf Man* were evocative and creepy, making it easy to believe a mild-mannered man like Larry Talbot could become a bloodthirsty creature at night.

In the fog-enshrouded woods, the Wolf Man pulls an unconscious Gwen toward him. Perhaps the cruelest aspect of the curse afflicting Larry Talbot was that it drove him to harm the ones he loved most.

*   *   *

That night, Gwen ventures to Talbot Castle to find Larry and beg him to stay. But before she reaches the castle, she meets the old gypsy woman. The gypsy woman tries to tell her what Larry has become, but Gwen does not believe her. Heartbroken, Gwen flees into the darkened forest.

The moon has risen, and a werewolf stalks the forest once again. After turning into the beast, Larry broke free from his bonds in Talbot Castle. Now he silently moves through the forest where he eyes the helpless Gwen.

Gwen tries to run, but she is not as fast as the monster. She screams as it bears down upon her. As the werewolf's hands are about to close around her neck, it is distracted by Sir John, who has been searching the woods as part of another hunting party. Consumed by a lust for blood, the inhuman thing that Larry has become charges at his father!

Sir John bravely faces the charging beast, the wolf's head cane gripped in his hand. As the monster attacks him, he brings the cane down, striking the creature again and again. Soon, the beast is silent, lying lifeless on the forest floor.

Larry's father looks down in horror as the monster slowly transforms back into his son. The gypsy woman comes from the woods and kneels next to Larry's lifeless body. She bends low and whispers to him:

The way you walked was thorny through no fault of your own, but as the rain enters the soil, the river enters the sea, so tears surround the predestined dead. Your suffering is over, my son. Now you will find peace.

After a few moments, the search party arrives and sees Larry's corpse. Thinking that he is a victim of the wolf, they quickly express their condolences to Sir John before running after their quarry.

Sir John, now childless, is left to contemplate the fact that perhaps there are greater mysteries in the world than he'd thought.

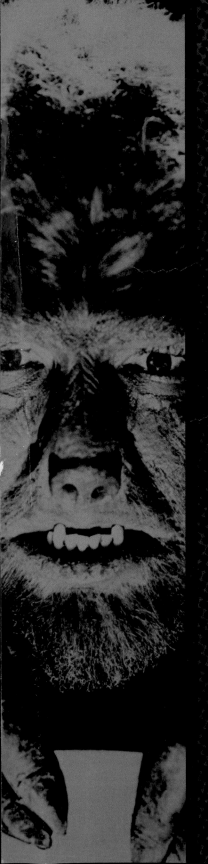

CHAPTER 2

BRINGING THE WOLF MAN TO LIFE

The idea of throwing off the constraints of the human form has captivated people for thousands of years. In fact, there are few cultures in the world that don't have some kind of myth about human beings transforming into animals. These legends live on in paintings, songs, and the folktales passed from one generation to the next. Each culture's legends are different, and many have been lost to time. One of these surviving legends, the legend of the werewolf, originated in Europe nearly 1,000 years ago.

Unlike the tragic creatures in Hollywood films, the werewolves of legend were bloodthirsty monsters of pure evil. Stories of werewolves slaughtering innocent people and robbing graves were common in the European countryside, where real wolves could be a threat to isolated villagers during the lean winter months. Hundreds of years later, a screenwriter named Curt Siodmak would take these legends and distill them into one of the greatest monster movies of all time.

The Wolf Man wasn't the first werewolf movie to come out of Hollywood, but it set an example that nearly all werewolf films that came after would imitate. *The Wolf Man* was made by Universal Studios in 1941, a time when World War II (1939–1945) was raging in Europe. *The Wolf Man* was a landmark horror film, and its eerie atmosphere and creepy plot spawned countless imitations. Most important, however, it introduced a monster to the world that, like all great monsters, refuses to die.

UNIVERSAL STUDIOS

In the 1930s, 1940s, and 1950s, Universal Studios released a number of monster movies that, today, are considered classics. *The Wolf Man* was just one of these films, and it stands beside *Frankenstein*, *Dracula*, and *The Creature from the Black Lagoon* in the pantheon of classic monster movies.

Despite its status as the definitive werewolf film since it first appeared in theaters in 1941, *The Wolf Man* was not the first werewolf movie ever made. That distinction

The iconic face of the Wolf Man leers out from this 1941 movie poster. Note that Universal has billed Lon Chaney Jr. as simply Lon Chaney—his father's famous name.

15

Werewolf of London featured a handsome British botanist named Dr. Wilfred Glendon (Henry Hull) and his attempts to cure his lycanthropy. The makeup design in *Werewolf of London* was slightly tamer than that of *The Wolf Man*. The monster looked less wild, and he stalked fog-enshrouded London dressed as a British gentleman.

belongs to a seldom-seen silent film called *The Werewolf*, released in the United States in 1913. Clocking in at a mere eighteen minutes, *The Werewolf* was only the tip of iceberg. The next werewolf movie, *Werewolf of London*, was released by Universal in 1935. The movie's plot involved a scientist who, while visiting Tibet, gets bitten by a werewolf. The scientist, played by Henry Hull, returns to London bearing the curse of the werewolf. *Werewolf of London* was good, but the studio thought that they could do more with their new monster.

CURT SIODMAK, SCREENWRITER

Universal felt that *Werewolf of London* could have done better both publicly and critically. Based on the success of its other monster movies, Universal knew that a werewolf story had the potential to be a blockbuster. When Universal picked up the wolf man story again, it hired screenwriter Curt Siodmak to pen the tale. Siodmak, a German Jew, had fled his homeland when the Nazi Party came to power. After spending some time in London, Siodmak made his way to the United States. In Germany, Siodmak had been a fairly well-known science fiction author, and Americans were receptive to his imaginative writing.

Besides presenting an entertaining supernatural yarn, Siodmak's finished screenplay included references to the Nazi's persecution of Jews. For instance, the fact that the

THE ORIGINAL TALE

The story for *The Wolf Man* was originally penned by a man named Robert Florey, who wanted to develop the movie into a vehicle for Boris Karloff, the star of *Frankenstein*. Florey's screenplay, if produced, would have been a much different movie than *The Wolf Man*. Florey's plot involved a boy living in the Swiss Alps who, after killing his parents, was raised by wolves. The studio thought that the script was too extreme and audiences would be turned off by it.

werewolf sees a star on his next victim alludes to the Nazi practice of making Jews wear a Star of David on their clothing at all times for identification purposes.

LON CHANEY JR.—THE WOLF MAN

Universal settled on Lon Chaney Jr. to bring life to its new monster. Chaney Jr. (born Creighton Chaney) was the son of legendary silent movie star Lon Chaney, who was affectionately known as the Man of a Thousand Faces. Lon Chaney Sr. was best known for his starring roles in classic suspense films such as *The Phantom of the Opera* and *The Hunchback of Notre Dame*.

Although Creighton had a good relationship with his father, the elder Chaney was determined to keep his son out of show business. As a result, Creighton unhappily worked

LON CHANEY: THE MAN OF A THOUSAND FACES

Born to parents who were both deaf-mutes, Lon Chaney became skilled at pantomime at an early age. This skill would serve him well in the silent films of the era, where much of the plot was conveyed by the actor's expressions. His ability to transform himself into horrifying characters made him one of the greatest stars of the silver screen, and he played a never-ending procession of monsters, maniacs, and gangsters. The gruesome makeup effects he designed for himself had a big impact on the monster makeup used in the Universal monster movies.

Lon Chaney Jr.'s *(left)* breakout Hollywood role was that of Lennie in *Of Mice and Men* (1939). The film was adapted from John Steinbeck's Depression-era novel about a mentally handicapped man (Lennie) and his friend George.

extremely dull nine-to-five jobs for a number of years. After his father succumbed to cancer in 1930, however, he decided that he'd had enough of the business world and that it was time to pursue his dream of being an actor.

It was difficult for young Creighton to find work at first. Hollywood studios wanted him to change his name to Lon Chaney Jr. so they could capitalize on his father's success. Creighton adamantly refused to do this for a number of years, wanting to make it as an actor on his own merit. It was tough going and resulted in few roles. On the verge of bankruptcy and with a family to support, Creighton finally caved in to studio pressure and changed his name to Lon Chaney Jr.

He soon landed a role as Lennie in the stage version of John Steinbeck's *Of Mice and Men* and was offered the same role in the film version. Universal sat up and took notice. In 1941, the studio pegged Chaney Jr. to play the lead role in its upcoming werewolf picture. Chaney Jr. would play the lead role as Larry Talbot, the man who succumbs to the curse of the werewolf. Chaney Jr. considered this his favorite role up until the day that he died. In fact, he played Larry Talbot in every sequel to the original film, truly making the tragic character his own.

FILMING DURING WARTIME

In 1941, Universal contracted director George Waggner to shoot its werewolf film. Waggner had directed a number of films, including a number of Westerns. His experienced direction put *The Wolf Man* head and shoulders above other fright flicks of the time. Waggner kept the action simple and emphasized the film's creepy atmosphere. By day, the sets looked like a quiet village, but by night the villages were eerie, with creeping fog and twisted trees looming out of the darkness.

The movie was shot almost entirely indoors among the quaint, rustic sets of Universal's "European Village" sound-stage. Universal recycled a lot of its sets in other films, and *The Wolf Man* was no exception. In the forest scenes, for instance, the production crew simply moved the trees around to make the landscape look different.

In Siodmak's original script, Talbot Castle was supposed to be located in Wales. However, in the final film version, the location of Talbot Castle is never revealed. The movie only hints that it is set in a small and mysterious land in Europe, a land where the supernatural still dwells.

In 1941, World War II was raging across Europe. Although the United States would not join the fight against Germany and the Axis powers until later that year, the war was on the minds of all American citizens. Universal realized that even the most terrifying monster movie would seem silly and pointless when compared to the horrors of battle. So, Universal carefully avoided mentioning any specifics that might relate to the war or any of the countries involved.

JACK PIERCE: MASTER OF MAKEUP

The Wolf Man's creative team was rounded out by makeup artist Jack Pierce. A visionary artist, he designed the makeup of all of the most famous Universal monsters, including Dracula, Frankenstein, and the Mummy. Pierce's talents at creating these visions set the standard for horror movies to come.

The first decision that Pierce faced for creating his were-wolf was how the creature should be designed. Should he be mostly wolflike, or should he retain human features? The design Pierce decided on was a combination of the two, allowing for maximum facial expressiveness by the actor. The

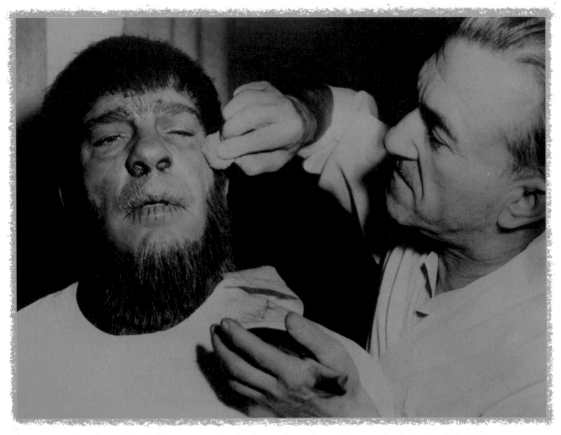

Makeup wizard Jack Pierce works to transform Lon Chaney Jr. into the Wolf Man. The long hours Chaney spent in the makeup chair led to some ill feelings between the two men. According to some people involved in the film, Pierce would unfavorably compare Chaney Jr. to his father.

important aspect of the Wolf Man, he felt, was that it was a monster with a distinct human side that should be allowed to show through the heavy makeup. The Wolf Man's face would evoke both fear and compassion in the audience.

Pierce built up Chaney's face with putty and mortician's wax, giving Chaney an overhanging brow and heavy cheekbones. To Chaney's face, Pierce glued strand after strand of yak hair, which he then singed with a curling iron to make it look more wild. The makeup took six hours to apply and two hours to remove.

For the transformation sequences, Pierce would apply a little bit of makeup, they'd film it, he'd apply a little more, they'd film it, and so on, creating the illusion of transformation. While it resulted in the most haunting scenes in the film, the process was extraordinarily tedious.

BEYOND THE WOLF MAN

Those who knew Lon Chaney Jr. remember him as a hard-working man who lived in the shadow of his father's success. Chaney Jr. got along well with everyone in the cast of *The Wolf Man*. This undoubtedly made the experience of shooting a little easier for some of the other actors who weren't accustomed to making monster movies.

Sequels to *The Wolf Man* were not quite so star-studded. They were also not as successful as the original. Audience interest in the Wolf Man waned, and Universal eventually retired its lupine monster after the comedy *Abbott and Costello Meet Frankenstein* was released in 1948. However, Lon Chaney Jr. would continue to work in Hollywood until his death in 1973, appearing in such films as *High Noon*, *The Defiant Ones*, and *The Haunted Palace*. Despite his extensive work as an actor, the name Lon Chaney Jr. would forever be synonymous to moviegoers with the character of the doomed Larry Talbot.

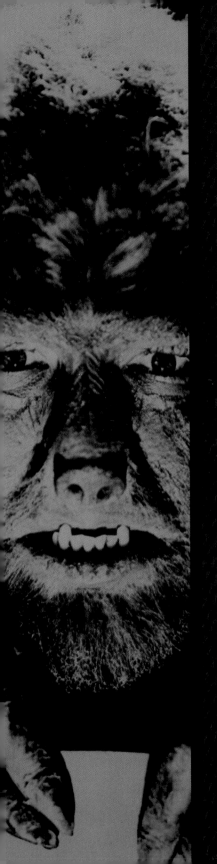

CHAPTER 3

WEREWOLF MYTHS

When interviewed, screenwriter Curt Siodmak insisted that he'd based *The Wolf Man* on ancient European werewolf myths. While this is partially true, Siodmak's screenplay owes relatively little to any actual legends or superstitions. Almost all modern werewolf movies follow the conventions Siodmak invented for the 1941 film, such as a werewolf's vulnerability to silver, a transformation triggered by the full moon, and the ability to pass along the curse through a bite.

However, the idea of human beings transforming into animals has existed for thousands of years. Many cultures developed tales and myths dealing with shape-shifting (assuming the shape and powers of animals). In ancient Greece, the god Zeus was said to be able to take on different forms, most famously that of a swan to seduce the human princess Leda. A popular Norse legend is that of the beserker, a warrior who went insane with bloodlust in battle, fighting with no regard for his own safety. Beserkers always wore bear or wolf skins, which were believed to give them their ferocious powers. In Japanese and Native American cultures, shape-shifting is often associated with various trickster gods.

ORIGINS OF THE WEREWOLF

The first recorded use of the word "werewolf" was in eleventh-century England during the Middle Ages, a dark period of European history from the fifth to fifteenth centuries. Religion and superstition tended to mix strangely in Europe during the Middle Ages. People did not know then what we know now about medicine, psychology, and science. Murderers,

This eighteenth-century engraving by B. Picart depicts the myth of Lycaon. In Greek mythology, Lycaon was a king of Arcadia who attempted to serve Zeus a slaughtered child as a sacrifice. As punishment, Zeus turned Lycaon into a wolf.

grave robbers, and the mentally ill were often believed to be possessed by supernatural forces. Many people were tortured, tried, and executed simply on the suspicion that they might be witches, werewolves, or posessed creatures in league with the devil. However, there was little evidence for the supposed crimes they were charged with, and their confessions were almost always extracted through crude torture. It wasn't long before werewolves went from being vague metaphoric figures to actual living beings in the popular imagination.

During the eleventh century, werewolves were symbolic of evil forces or entities that would prey on a priest's or bishop's congregation. To religious leaders, the sin that might tempt churchgoers was as dangerous as a wolf to a flock of sheep. Werewolves represented the kind of temptations that could throw an otherwise devout parishioner's soul into mortal peril.

By the fourteenth century, werewolves were considered to be direct allies of Satan in Christian Europe. Some people thought that Satan provided his followers with a salve, or ointment, that would turn them into wolves. This salve was rumored to consist of the plants henbane and belladonna, opium, bat's blood, the boiled fat of an unbaptized child, and other unsavory ingredients. After its transformation, the werewolf would carry out Satan's evil work on Earth.

THE FIRST WEREWOLF?

The first person ever identified as a werewolf was a man named Peter Stubbe, who lived in Germany in the sixteenth century. Under torture, Stubbe confessed that the devil had granted him the ability to turn into a wolf, and he claimed to be guilty of a string of grisly, cannibalistic murders. Torture was commonplace in those days, and there is no way of knowing if Stubbe was actually guilty of the crimes he confessed to. Stubbe was brutally executed, and his head was impaled on a tall pole with a woodcut of a wolf nailed to it to show the townspeople what shape he had assumed when committing his crimes.

These medieval woodcuts show witches taking on the forms of animals, particularly wolves. People believed to be witches were mercilessly persecuted in Europe during medieval times. If convicted of being a witch, a person could expect to be burned at the stake, crushed to death by stones, drowned, hanged, or be subject to any number of other gruesome deaths.

Other people believed that werewolves could change between human and wolf forms at will or that transformation required a belt made from the skin of a wolf or a bear or skin from the corpse of an executed murderer.

Local werewolf superstitions varied from region to region. As the Bible is devoid of any references to werewolves, the Catholic Church did not take an official stance on their nature. Still, people generally agreed that werewolves had wolflike characteristics that could be detected even when they were in human form. These included pronounced eyebrows that met at the middle of the forehead, an extra long ring finger, and a reddish tint to the eyes and teeth. Many people also believed that werewolves hated sunlight and that they were unable to cry.

MODERN MEDICAL CASES

One modern explanation for these "werewolf" symptoms is a disease called congenital porphyria. This disease causes the cartilage of the face and the bones of the hands and feet to deteriorate. It also results in extreme sensitivity to sunlight, which can cause skin lesions to appear, as well as a tendency for the teeth to darken.

Besides the disfigurement it causes to the body, porphyria can also affect the brain of the afflicted. People with porphyria can suffer from epilepsy, severe depression, and sometimes psychosis. Because of their aversion to sunlight, people with porphyria probably only ventured out at night. Some historians think that those who suffered from this disease may have inspired the first werewolf myths.

Other diseases also may have contributed to the myth of werewolves. Chief among these are the diseases hypertrichosis and rabies. Hypertrichosis is an extremely rare condition that results in a full-body coating of hair, including the face. In nineteenth-century England, people with hypertrichosis were often exhibited as sideshow freaks.

Rabies, on the other hand, is still a common disease. It is passed from one mammal to another through the transmission of bodily fluids, and it causes high fever, sore throat, violent irritability, insomnia, and sometimes hallucinations. Rabies also causes animals to become furious, attacking and biting anything and anybody who crosses their path. It can also have a similar effect on humans. Rabies is fatal unless treated, and it was greatly feared before a cure for it was discovered in 1885 by Louis Pasteur.

Modern cases of lycanthropy are rare and usually involve people with serious psychological problems. Today's lycanthropes suffer from delusions leading them to believe they are werewolves, usually brought on by heavy drug use or severe psychological trauma. Even though we are no longer afraid that our communities might be set upon by werewolves, they still feature prominently in our cultural imagination.

CHAPTER 4

THE INFLUENCE OF THE WOLF MAN

The Wolf Man became one of the most popular monster movies ever released. After its release Universal quickly realized that its creation had a considerable amount of moneymaking potential. When horror fans demanded to see more of the Wolf Man, the studio was more than happy to comply.

LARRY TALBOT LIVES ON

When it was released in 1941, *The Wolf Man* did well enough at the box office to warrant the monster's appearance in four more films, all featuring Lon Chaney Jr. The first of these, *Frankenstein Meets the Wolf Man* (released in 1943), marked the first time that two classic Universal monsters faced off. In the film, Larry Talbot's tomb is broken into by grave robbers, and he is mysteriously awakened from the dead by their intrusion. Not wanting to harm any more innocent people, Larry spends the movie trying to die and stay dead. Eventually, a scientist devises a plan by which Larry's life force will be transferred into the inanimate corpse of the Frankenstein monster. Unfortunately, the experiment is a failure. The movie ends with an epic battle between the monsters, who meet their end when the castle they are in comes tumbling down around them.

The next film Larry Talbot appears in is *House of Frankenstein* (1944). In this horror flick, Larry, Count Dracula, and Frankenstein's monster are brought back to life by a deranged scientist. The scientist, played by Boris Karloff, has a plan to switch Larry's brain with that of one of his assistants. In his new, mortal body, Larry will presumably be able to die of natural causes.

The stitched-together hands of Frankenstein's monster close around the neck of the Wolf Man. *Frankenstein Meets the Wolf Man* marked the first time Universal would pit two of its most famous monsters against one another. For the film, Lon Chaney Jr. reprised his role as the Wolf Man while Bela Lugosi played Frankenstein's monster.

Before this sinister experiment can be seen through, Larry's girlfriend decides to take matters into her own hands. She shoots Larry with a silver bullet, a tried and true method of destroying any werewolf.

Any werewolf, that is, except for one as profitable as the Wolf Man. With box-office receipts grossly outweighing a logical storyline, Universal brought back the seemingly immortal Larry Talbot for an appearance in the film *House of Dracula* (1945). Still wanting to cure his lycanthropy, Larry consults a doctor. The doctor explains that his transformations into a werewolf are not really caused by the full moon or wolfsbane, but rather by a bizarre physical condition. Although this is perhaps even less believable than a supernatural curse, it does present an easy cure: surgery. Larry watches the full moon rise at the end of the film, thrilled that he remains a man.

Larry's final appearance as the Wolf Man came in *Abbott and Costello Meet Frankenstein* (released in 1948). Bud Abbott and Lou Costello were one of the most famous comic duos of the day. They made several zany films that featured Universal's classic monsters. During the hijinx that ensues in *Abbott and Costello Meet Frankenstein*, Larry meets his end by leaping over a balcony in pursuit of Count Dracula. A silly parody of Universal horror movies, *Abbott and Costello Meet Frankenstein* signaled the end of most of the famous Universal monsters. The once horrifying creatures from *Dracula*, *Frankenstein*, and *The Wolf Man* were each used for comic effect to rake in money for the Abbott and Costello series. Chaney Jr. would act in dozens of films before his death, but he would never star as Larry Talbot again. Amid the laughter of *Abbott and Costello Meet Frankenstein*, the Wolf Man had finally managed to find peace.

MONSTER MANIA

In the decades that followed the Wolf Man's disappearance from the silver screen in 1948, an entire horror-movie culture was born in the United States. Movie studios were churning out hundreds of low-budget monster movies to make a quick buck. Many middle-class families could now afford to own a television set, providing a new market for monster movies and their spin-offs. Classic (and not-so-classic) horror films became a favorite feature on late-night television and were often presented by wacky horror hosts such as Zacherle and Vampira. Television shows like *The Munsters* (1964–1966) and *The Addams Family* (1964–1966) sprang up, unleashing a whole new crew of ghouls on an unsuspecting television audience.

In 1958, a man named Forrest J. Ackerman launched a magazine called *Famous Monsters of Filmland*, which featured interviews with and articles on the stars of the great horror films. Gruesome comic books such as *Tales from the Crypt*, *Vault of Horror*, and *Haunt of Fear* hit the newsstands. These titles, published by EC Comics, contained grisly stories of murder and revenge. The illustrations in these comics, drawn by artists such as Wallace Wood and "Ghastly" Graham Ingles, were often so sickening that they would not have passed a movie censor.

By then, monster mania was producing all types of personalities and products. A gruff-voiced radio DJ named Wolfman Jack emerged from Brooklyn, New York, to become a national celebrity as he spun rock 'n' roll records for kids all over North America. Bobby Pickett released his classic song "Monster Mash" in 1962, which became a gigantic hit. Other rock 'n' rollers, such as Screaming Jay Hawkins and Screamin' Lord Sutch, recorded songs with horror themes while wearing ghoulish makeup.

THE ATOMIC AGE

Despite the fact that the Wolf Man was alive in music, comic books, and magazines, there were few good werewolf movies made through the 1950s, 1960s, and 1970s. As the world's political climate changed, old-fashioned monsters quickly went out of style. Following World War II, the United States and the Soviet Union emerged as the world's two superpowers. The two countries stockpiled atomic weapons, and the threat of nuclear war shadowed the world for decades. The very real threat of all-out atomic destruction became the new bogeyman, keeping children (and their parents) awake at night. Atomic-age monstrosities such as Godzilla, the Crawling Eye, the Thing, and others dominated the horror market.

It was during this time that science fiction films also rose to prominence.

Michael Landon, still wearing his letterman jacket, stars in *I Was a Teenage Werewolf*. A movie aimed at a growing teenage audience, *I Was a Teenage Werewolf* features a young high school student suffering from low self-esteem.

Doing away with the haunted castles and cobweb-covered crypts of *Dracula* and *The Wolf Man*, science fiction films cast an eye toward the future. The cerebral nature of many science fiction films made horror movies such as *I Was a Teenage Werewolf* (1957) look silly and old-fashioned.

THE HAMMER REVIVAL

As classic monsters seemed to disappear in America, a small British film studio was reviving the genre across the Atlantic. Hammer Studios produced many updated versions of the classic Universal monster movies that starred Count Dracula, Frankenstein's monster, and the

Hammer Studios, a movie studio based in the United Kingdom, threw its hat in the ring with *Curse of the Werewolf*, starring Oliver Reed. Hammer became famous for its colorful and gory adaptations of classic monster movies.

Wolf Man. However, unlike the Universal monster movies, the Hammer films were filmed in breathtaking color, capturing the horror and blood of these tales with updated story lines. Today, the Hammer monster movies are considered classics and include *The Brides of Dracula*, *The Curse of Frankenstein*, and *The Mummy*. The Wolf Man even got his own Hammer film in 1961's *Curse of the Werewolf*, starring Oliver Reed.

But by the 1970s, werewolf films were becoming an endangered species in America. It wasn't until the early 1980s that a new crop of fearsome films dealing with lycanthropy hit the theaters stateside.

THE NEW BREED

The two films that probably did the most for the revival of werewolf movies were *An American Werewolf in London* (1981) and *The Howling* (1980). Since the release of these movies, and their box-office success, werewolves began making appearances on the big screen on a pretty regular basis.

In *An American Werewolf in London*, directed by John Landis, a young man named David (David Naughton) and his friend Jack (Griffin Dunne) go hiking through the foggy English countryside when they are attacked by a wolf and both are bitten. Jack is killed, and David must live with the curse of a werewolf. He is visited by Jack from beyond the grave, falls in love with the nurse (Jenny Agutter) taking care of him, and stalks the city during the night as a monster. Keeping very close to the plot of *The Wolf Man*, *An American Werewolf in London* is a very skillful mixture of horror, gore, and humor.

The Howling, on the other hand, comes off almost as a grim, fast-paced crime thriller. Directed by Joe Dante, it involves a television anchorwoman named Karen White (Dee Wallace) who is staying at a nature retreat in northern California with her husband. She is trying to recover from a traumatic encounter with a murderer, but finds herself in even

Through the use of latex special effects, actor David Naughton transforms into a hideous monster in *An American Werewolf in London*. As nightmarish as the transformation scenes in *American Werewolf* are, the film is filled with humor, provoking as many laughs as cringes from audiences.

worse trouble. The people who live at the retreat seem strange, and she soon discovers that they are actually a community of werewolves. After one of them seduces her husband, he, too, becomes a werewolf. Before she can escape, she is bitten and doomed to become a werewolf as well.

In 1997 a sequel to *An American Werewolf in London* was released as *An American Werewolf in Paris*, starring

Unlike *An American Werewolf in London,* *The Howling* made little use of humor. Here, a snarling werewolf advances on a screaming victim.

Tom Everett Scott and Julie Delpy. Despite the fact that *An American Werewolf in Paris* featured state-of-the-art special effects, it did not have the impact of its predecessor.

The Howling spawned a number of sequels as well. What made the originals stand out, aside from the fact that they were good, scary films, was the revolutionary special effects they employed. Utilizing latex, inflatable air bladders (to make skin transform), and inventive camera techniques, these production teams created horrifying werewolves that made Jack Pierce's Wolf Man look like a harmless puppy in comparison. Hydraulic mechanisms and latex masks bulged and stretched, accompanied by the sound of bones snapping and tendons stretching. Horror fans all over the world cringed when they saw these transformation scenes for the first time. Special effects had finally found a way to make werewolves look as horrifying as the audience's worst nightmares.

THE WEREWOLF LIVES ON

In the last ten years or so, computer-generated imagery, or CGI, has become increasingly prevalent in horror and science fiction films. The werewolf of *An American Werewolf in Paris* was generated with CGI, as were the werewolves from more recent movies such as *Van Helsing* (2004), *Underworld* (2003), and a French film called *Le Pactes de Loups* (Brotherhood of the Wolf), released in 2001. Although things can be done with computers that are not possible in real life, some people say that digital effects don't look as scary as those done with makeup and latex applications. There are some monster movie fans who would even argue that no movie werewolf has looked as good as Lon Chaney Jr.'s original Wolf Man, covered in mortician's wax and yak hair, as he crept through the fog of a cemetery at night.

Year after year, werewolf movies are released around the globe for movie fans hungry for horror. At this point, so many werewolf movies have been made in so many different countries that it is doubtful anyone has seen them all. *The Wolf Man* may not have been the first werewolf movie, but it provided the mold from which all werewolf films that followed it were cast. *The Wolf Man* has been made fun of, paid homage to, and blatantly ripped off over the decades. However, the most important legacy of *The Wolf Man* is that it has spawned a monster that will captivate and terrify us for generations to come.

FILMOGRAPHY

Werewolf of London (1935) The direct precursor to *The Wolf Man*. Henry Hull plays a man infected by the bite of a werewolf during a trip to Tibet.

The Wolf Man (1941) The movie that defined Lon Chaney Jr.'s career. *The Wolf Man* is considered to be the ultimate werewolf movie.

Frankenstein Meets the Wolf Man (1943) The first time two Universal monsters faced off on screen.

House of Frankenstein (1944) Larry Talbot comes back, looking for a way to cure his affliction.

House of Dracula (1945) Larry Talbot comes back, yet again. By this time, Curt Siodmak was long gone, and the story suffers because of it.

Abbott and Costello Meet Frankenstein (1948) Chaney has a small part in this film, which marks a bizarre end to one of Universal's most lucrative horror franchises.

I Was a Teenage Werewolf (1957) Michael Landon stars as a moody teenager who is transformed into a werewolf by his doctor.

The Curse of the Werewolf (1961) Set in Spain, this movie features Oliver Reed as a man born into the life of a werewolf.

The Howling (1980) Directed by Joe Dante, *The Howling* featured suspenseful horror and incredible special effects.

An American Werewolf in London (1981) Written and directed by John Landis, *An American Werewolf in London* features great special effects, horror, and dark comedy.

Silver Bullet (1985) A teenager in a small town tries to figure out who among the townspeople is a werewolf in this adaptation of a Stephen King story.

Teen Wolf (1985) Michael J. Fox plays a teenager who has the power to change himself into a werewolf. He uses this power to dominate on the basketball court.

Monster Squad (1987) Dracula comes up with a plan to revive the Mummy, Frankenstein's monster, the Wolf Man, and the creature from the Black Lagoon. A fun, campy movie.

An American Werewolf in Paris (1997) The belated sequel to *An American Werewolf in London*, *An American Werewolf in Paris* relied heavily on CGI effects for its monster.

Brotherhood of the Wolf (2001) This French film, set on the eve of the French Revolution, contains inventive cinematography and a novel approach to the old monster.

Underworld (2003) This modern action movie pits vampires against werewolves.

Van Helsing (2004) The famous vampire hunter is revived and updated, facing down Dracula, Frankenstein's monster, and the Wolf Man.

GLOSSARY

Axis powers The alliance between Germany, Japan, and Italy during World War II.

belladonna Also called deadly nightshade, belladonna is a flowering plant with extremely poisonous berries.

epilepsy A medical condition resulting in attacks of uncontrollable muscle spasms.

henbane A poisonous flowering herb.

homage A tribute.

latex A pliable kind of rubber often used for special effects.

lupine Wolflike; from *lupus*, the Latin word for "wolf."

mortician's wax Putty used by morticians for purposes of reconstructing a corpse's features. It is often used by makeup artists to alter an actor's features.

mute Unable to speak.

Nazi A member of the Nazi Party, which came to power in Germany in 1933 and collapsed in 1945. The Nazis committed horrible acts of genocide against gypsies, Jews, and other ethnic groups they found "undesirable."

opium A drug distilled from poppy seeds that can distort the perceptions of the user.

pantheon A group of important people or things.

pentagram A five-pointed star inside of a circle. The pentagram has different meanings in different cultures, although an inverted pentagram is often considered to be a symbol of evil.

sideshow An attraction at many traveling carnivals where people could pay to see people with unusual physical characteristics.

wolfsbane A poisonous herb with yellow flowers commonly found in Europe.

FOR MORE INFORMATION

American Museum of the Moving Image
35th Avenue at 36th Street
Astoria, NY 11106
(718) 784-0077
Web site: http://www.AMMI.org

American Film Institute
The John F. Kennedy Center for the Performing Arts
Washington, DC 20566
(202) 833-AFIT (2348)
Web site: http://www.AFI.com

WEB SITES

Due to the changing nature of Internet links, the Rosen Publishing Group, Inc., has developed an online list of Web sites related to the subject of this book. This site is updated regularly. Please use this link to access the list:

http://www.rosenlinks.com/famm/mewm

FOR FURTHER READING

Brunas, John, Michael Brunas, and Tom Weaver. *Universal Horrors: The Studio's Classic Films, 1931–1946.* Jefferson, NC: McFarland & Company, 1990.

Skal, David J. *The Monster Show: A Cultural History of Horror.* London: Faber & Faber, 2001.

BIBLIOGRAPHY

Constable, George, ed. *The Enchanted World: Night Creatures*. Chicago: Time Life Books, 1985.

Constable, George. *Transformations: Mysteries of the Unknown*. Chicago: Time Life Books, 1989.

Husse, Roy, and T. J. Ross, eds. *Focus on the Horror Film*. Englewood Cliffs, NJ: Prentice Hall, Inc., 1972.

Monster by Moonlight! The Immortal Saga of "The Wolf Man." Directed by David J. Skal, 1999. Universal Studios Home Video.

Newman, Kim. *Nightmare Movies: A Critical Guide to Contemporary Horror Films*. New York: Harrows Books, 1988.

Otten, Charlotte F. *A Lycanthropy Reader: Werewolves in Western Culture*. Syracuse, NY: Syracuse University Press, 1986.

Sierchio, Patrick. *Interview with a Wolf Man*. Accessed March 2004 (http://www.wga.org/WrittenBy/1299/siodmak.html).

Skal, David J. *The Monster Show*. New York: W. W. Norton Company, 1993.

Summers, Montague. *The Werewolf*. New York: Bell Publishing Company, 1966.

INDEX

ABOUT THE AUTHOR

R. K. Renfield is a freelance writer who lives in New York State.

PHOTO CREDITS

Cover, pp. 1, 12, 31, 34 © Underwood & Underwood/Corbis; pp. 4, 5, 7, 10, 14, 15, 22, 24, 30, 35, 37, 38 © The Everett Collection; p. 16 © Bettmann/Corbis; p. 19 © John Springer Collection/Corbis; p. 25 © Historical Picture Archive/Corbis; p. 27 © Stapleton Collection/Corbis.

Designer: Thomas Forget; Editor: Charles Hofer